How to Help Your Child Learn, Think, and Succeed Independently

From Curiosity to Leadership:

A Parent's Guide to Raising Confident, Independent Learners

Anil Kumar Khandelwal

How to Help Your Child Learn, Think, and Succeed Independently
From Curiosity to Leadership – A Parent's Guide to Raising Confident, Independent Learners

ISBN: 978-1-0693862-5-0 (Paperback)
ISBN: 978-1-0693862-6-7 (eBook)

Published by
Anil Kumar Khandelwal

For more information:
globalmathinstitute.com
YouTube: @MathematicsTutor

Printed in Canada

Foreword

A note from Vishu G., School Principal, New York City

Having known Anil K. as a family friend, mentor, and coach, I have seen firsthand the impact of his approach on children and families.

The strategies shared in this book are ready to implement today
and are an investment in your child's future.

When a child is provided with a safe space—
when they feel secure in the presence and guidance of their parents, they begin to blossom as learners, even beyond the influence of their favorite teacher.

Months, sometimes years later,
they will remember those quiet, meaningful moments—
the gentle, non-judgmental conversations at home.

In those moments, learning was not just about mathematics.
It was about thinking, understanding, and feeling heard.

And that experience builds something deeper—trust.

Over time, that trust extends beyond academics.
It shapes how they make decisions and approach challenges.

As you read this book, take time to absorb and apply these ideas.

You are not just helping your child learn.
You are becoming a trusted guide and
a coach — not just for now but through their adulthood.

And that is not only a possibility—
it can be your family's reality.

— *Vishu G.*
School Principal, New York City

Preface

I am a parent first
and then a mentor, educator, or guide.

A child sits with a book open...
not confused, but waiting.
Waiting to be told what to do next.
That moment changed everything for me.

Where This Journey Began

My journey into teaching did not begin in a classroom.
It began at home.
There was a time when my own child—once confident and capable—began to struggle.
Not because of a lack of ability,
but because something deeper had changed.
The joy of learning was no longer present.
As a parent, I found myself asking:
What changed?
How can I help?
Am I doing enough... or doing too much?
These are not just questions—
they are experiences shared by parents everywhere.

A Turning Point

In that moment, I made a decision that changed everything.
I stepped away from my professional career
to understand how children truly learn—
not only academically, but emotionally and mentally.
What began with one child soon grew.
Students from the neighborhood joined,
and over time, this became a global journey—

working with learners across countries, cultures, and educational systems.

What Became Clear

Across these experiences, one truth became clear:
Children do not struggle because they cannot learn.
They struggle because the way they are guided
does not always support how they learn.

About This Book

This book is not theory.
It is built on real experiences and real transformations—
what works in classrooms and at home.
In a world of instant answers,
this book focuses on building lasting understanding.
You do not need to change everything.
Sometimes, a small shift creates the biggest difference.

A Personal Note

This is not about raising perfect students.
It is about raising:

- Confident learners
- Thoughtful individuals
- Independent thinkers

When we guide differently,
children learn differently.
The journey of learning begins at home.

In quiet moments—
a pause before helping,
a question instead of an instruction—
a child begins to think.
And that changes everything

Before You Begin — A Thinking Exercise

Pause Before You Start
Every journey begins with awareness.

Before you begin reading this book,
take a moment to reflect.
Words shape how we think.
And how we think shapes how we guide.

Below are groups of words often seen in learning and parenting.
Some support growth.
Some unknowingly limit it.
There are no right or wrong answers—yet.
Simply respond based on your current thinking.
By the end of this book,
you may see them very differently.

How to Use This Exercise
For each group of words:

- Circle words you believe support learning
- Cross words you feel may limit learning
- Leave blank if you are unsure

Do not overthink.
Trust your instinct.
After each exercise, you will be guided to specific chapters that help you explore these ideas more deeply.

EXERCISE 1 — Learning Approach
(Understanding the Problem — Chapters 1–3)

Curiosity	Memorizing	Discovery	Results
Marks	Questions	Performance	Why
Exploration	Speed	Trial	Practice
Completion	Thinking	Answers	Steps
Understanding	Instructions	Process	Accuracy

EXERCISE 2 — Guidance vs Pressure

(Changing the Approach — Chapters 4–6)

Guidance	Monitoring	Patience	Judgment
Pressure	Encouragement	Deadlines	Listening
Support	Comparison	Freedom	Correction
Control	Conversation	Expectations	Connection
Trust	Instructions	Safety	Evaluation

EXERCISE 3 — Habits and Learning

(Building Effective Systems — Chapters 7–9)

Consistency	Repetition	Engaging	Effort
Motivation	Recall	Focus	Strategy
Routine	Rereading	Distraction	Understanding
Cramming	Explanation	Planning	Shortcuts
Reflection	Absorbing	Guessing	Clarity

EXERCISE 4 — Growth and Outcomes

(Transformation — Chapters 10–12)

Mistakes	Fear	Challenge	Reflection
Failure	Confidence	Improvement	Independence
Feedback	Avoidance	Comparison	Dependence
Perfection	Risk	Self-belief	Leadership
Growth	Comfort	Judgment	Performance

Connecting the Words to the Journey

As you move through the chapters,
you may begin to notice patterns.
Words start to shift.

From → To

- Marks → Curiosity
- Pressure → Guidance
- Dependence → Independence
- Memorizing → Thinking
- Performance → Leadership

This is not just a change in words.

It is a change in:

- Thinking
- Approach
- Actions

And ultimately—
a change in your child's learning journey.

A Final Thought Before You Begin

This is not a test.
It is a starting point.
Return to these words
after completing the book.
You may find:

- Some words have changed meaning
- Some have become more important
- Some now guide your decisions

And that is where transformation begins.

Student & Parent Voices

Real journeys. Real growth. Real impact.

Behind every concept learned...
is a story of change.
Not just in marks,
but in confidence, thinking, and independence.

A Parent's Perspective

"As a parent, I am deeply grateful for the impact Anil has had on my children—Melisa, Joseph, and Nicholas—throughout their IB Mathematics journey.

What stood out was not just his ability to explain difficult concepts clearly, but the way he helped them think. With a structured approach, patience, and genuine care, he guided them to understand—not just memorize.

Over time, I saw a transformation:

- From hesitation to confidence
- From dependence to independence
- From completing work to truly understanding it

Melisa went on to excel in IB Mathematics and is now in medical school.

Joseph and Nicholas are both succeeding in university with the same strong foundation.

What makes Anil different is that his support goes beyond academics.

He builds thinking, confidence, and discipline—skills that stay with students long after exams are over.

He is not just a tutor.

He is a mentor who genuinely invests in each child's growth.

I would strongly recommend him to any parent who wants not only better results,

but a lasting change in how their child learns."

— Mariana Spognardi & Family

What These Stories Show

Across different students and backgrounds, a common pattern emerges:

- When guidance changes, learning changes
- When pressure reduces, confidence grows
- When thinking is encouraged, results improve

These are not isolated successes.
They are outcomes of a different approach to learning.

More Than Results

These journeys are not just about:

- Higher grades
- Academic success

They are about:

- Developing confidence
- Building independent thinking
- Creating lifelong learners

Because true success is not measured only by results—
but by who the child becomes in the process.

A Quiet Reminder

Every child has potential.
Sometimes, they do not need more instruction—
they need better guidance.
And when that shift happens,
growth becomes natural.

Behind every concept learned... is a story of growth.

Table of Contents

Introduction — From Curiosity to Leadership

Every journey begins with a question.

A child sits with a book open...
not confused —
but waiting.

Waiting to be told what to do next.

A Question Worth Asking

What if the way we are helping children learn
is not fully working?

Across homes and classrooms, a common pattern exists.

Children are:

- Attending school
- Completing homework
- Preparing for tests

Yet many parents notice:

- Lack of interest
- Dependence on reminders
- Fear of making mistakes
- Inconsistent results

This often results in frustration.

Not because children are not capable,
but because something in the process is missing.

The Missing Link

Most learning systems focus on:

- Content
- Completion
- Performance

But they often overlook:

- Curiosity
- Thinking
- Ownership

Over time, learning becomes mechanical.
Tasks are completed...
but understanding remains shallow.

This book is about shifting from pressure to purpose.

What This Book Will Help You Do

This book is designed to help you:

- Build curiosity instead of chasing marks
- Replace pressure with guidance
- Develop independent learning habits
- Strengthen understanding and confidence
- Turn mistakes into opportunities
- Move from average performance to meaningful growth

And most importantly—
raise children who think.

A Different Way to Look at Learning

Learning is not just about:

- Getting the right answer
- Finishing tasks
- Scoring higher

It is about:

- Asking better questions
- Understanding deeply
- Applying confidently

When children learn how to think,
they learn how to succeed.

How to Use This Book

Each chapter is designed to be:

- Simple
- Reflective
- Actionable

You will find:

- Key ideas
- Real-life insights
- Reflection prompts
- Practical steps

Read one chapter at a time,
or return to sections as needed.

A Note to Parents

You do not need to know everything.
You do not need all the answers.
Your role is not to teach everything.
Your role is to guide.
The right guidance creates the right environment.
And the right environment shapes learning.

The Journey Ahead

This book follows a simple path:

1. Understanding the problem
2. Changing the approach
3. Building effective habits
4. Creating transformation
5. Moving beyond success

> From curiosity...
> to confidence...
> to leadership.

A Final Thought Before You Begin

Every child can learn.

The real question is:
How are we guiding them?
Begin with one small shift:

- One question instead of an instruction
- One pause before helping
- One moment of trust

Note:

In this book, the term "*marks*" is used. In some regions, this is referred to as "*grades*." Both terms represent the same idea.

Change the way we guide—and everything changes.

1 — I Am a Parent First

*Sometimes, learning doesn't change —
the experience of learning does.*

A Small Shift That Changes Everything

Most parents try to help their children learn—but unknowingly make it harder.

One evening, I sat beside my child as she worked on a problem she usually solved with confidence. Gradually, something began to feel different.

Not confusion, but hesitation.

There was no failure.
No major setback.
And yet something had quietly changed.
The joy of learning was missing.

At first, I responded in the usual way—
more reminders, more instructions, more effort.

But nothing improved.

That is when I understood:
This is not just about learning.
It is about how we guide.

The Hidden Mistake

We often believe helping means:

- Giving instructions
- Monitoring closely
- Ensuring completion

But to a child, this may feel like:

- Pressure
- Constant evaluation
- Loss of ownership

Learning slowly shifts from exploration to expectation.

Example: A parent gave step-by-step instructions for every question, and the child stopped trying without being told what to do.

Pressure vs Guidance

Pressure says:

- Finish this
- Do it correctly
- Do not make mistakes

Guidance says:

- Let us understand this
- What do you think?
- Try again—what changed?

This shift may seem small,
but it changes everything.

What Children Really Need

Children are naturally curious.
They explore, question, and discover.

But when learning becomes focused only on:

- Grades or Marks
- Speed
- Completion

Curiosity fades
and is replaced by compliance.

Compliance is not learning.

Example: A child eager to try new ideas began waiting for instructions, after learning that only correct answers were valued.

A Different Starting Point

Before being a teacher,
before being a mentor,
we are parents first.

Parenting is not about control.
It is about connection.

One of the simplest ways to build that connection
is through everyday family moments.

A few minutes together—
a conversation at dinner,
a short story before bedtime—
can make a lasting difference.

When children share how their day was,
what they enjoyed,
or what they are grateful for,
they begin to feel heard and understood.

These are not just routines.
They are moments of trust.

And when trust is built at home,
children carry that confidence into their learning.

When children feel supported, they take risks.
When they take risks, they learn.

Reflection

- When does my child feel confident?
- When do they hesitate?
- Am I guiding or controlling?

Try This (Simple Shift)

- Replace one instruction with a question
  Instead of: "Do this step"
  Ask: "What would you try next?"

- Replace one correction with a pause
  Give 5–10 seconds before speaking

- Replace one reminder with a conversation
  "How are you planning to finish this?"

Key Takeaway

> Learning does not grow under pressure.
> It grows through connection, curiosity, and confidence.

What This Means

- Children learn best when they feel supported, not controlled
- Too many instructions can reduce ownership
- Pressure reduces curiosity and engagement
- Guidance encourages thinking and confidence
- Connection is the foundation of meaningful learning

Connection comes before correction.

2 — Curiosity vs Grades

Sometimes, marks improve,
but understanding does not.

What if We're Focusing on the Wrong Thing?
What if grades are not the real problem,
but the focus is?

A Quiet Shift

In many homes, learning is measured by one thing:
Grades.

- "How much did you get?"
- "Why not higher?"
- "What happened here?"

These questions come from care.
But over time, something subtle happens.

Learning becomes **performance-driven**.
And curiosity begins to fade.

When "Why" Disappears

Children naturally learn by asking:

- Why is this happening?
- How does this work?
- What happens if I try this?

This is where real learning often begins.
But when grades become the focus, questions change:

- Will this be on the test?
- What steps should I remember?
- What is the fastest way to answer?

When "why" disappears,
learning becomes a task.

The Illusion of Progress

Grades can improve without understanding.
A child may:

- Memorize steps
- Practice repeatedly
- Perform well on tests

But struggle when:

- The question changes
- A new idea appears
- Thinking is required

It looks like progress,
but the foundation is weak.

Example: A student completed all the practice questions correctly but could not explain why the method works.

A Powerful Shift

Instead of asking:
"Did you get full score?"
Try asking:

- What did you discover today?
- What confused you?
- What did you enjoy learning?

This shift changes the message:
Learning matters more than performance.

Why Curiosity Matters

Curiosity leads to:

- Deeper understanding
- Better retention
- Stronger problem-solving
- Independent thinking

Curious learners:

- Explore beyond the textbook
- Make connections
- Ask better questions

And when this happens,
grades follow naturally.

The Role of Parents

Parents shape learning—not by doing more,
but by guiding better.
When children feel:

- Safe to ask questions
- Comfortable making mistakes
- Encouraged to explore

They take ownership.
And ownership leads to growth.

Reflection

Pause and think:

- Do I talk more about grades or learning?
- How often do I ask "why" questions?
- Does my child feel safe asking questions?

Try This (Simple Shift)

Over the next few days:

- Ask one curiosity-based question daily
  Example: "What surprised you today?"

- Appreciate thinking—not just correct answers
  Example: "I like how you approached this."

- Encourage your child to ask questions
  Example: "What would you like to understand better?"

- Observe what changes.

Key Takeaway

> Curiosity is the starting point of learning.
> Marks are a reflection—not the goal.

What This Reveals

- Focusing only on grades reduces curiosity
- True learning begins with questions
- Memorization without understanding is fragile
- Curiosity strengthens thinking and retention
- When understanding grows, results follow naturally

Do not chase grades.
Build curiosity—and improvement will follow.

3 — Why Interest Fades

Interest does not disappear suddenly.
It fades when meaning is lost.

It Doesn't Happen Overnight

Children don't lose interest overnight,
they lose meaning.

A Quiet Change

Every child begins with curiosity.
They explore.
They ask questions.
They engage with excitement.
But over time, something changes.
Not suddenly.
Not dramatically.
Quietly.

What Really Changes

When interest fades, we often assume:

- The child is distracted
- The child lacks focus
- The child needs discipline

But the truth is deeper.
Interest does not disappear.
It is replaced.
Replaced by:

- Pressure
- Repetition without understanding
- Fear of making mistakes

When learning loses meaning,
interest fades.

From Curiosity to Compliance

At first, children learn because they **want to**.

Later, many learn because they **have to**.

The change is subtle, but important:

- From curiosity → performance
- From exploration → instruction

As a result, learning shifts toward compliance.

And while compliance may produce results,
it weakens learning over time.

A child completing tasks
is not always a child learning.

The Role of Pressure

Pressure often begins with good intentions.
Parents want:

- Better results
- Stronger performance
- Academic success

But too much pressure creates:

- Anxiety
- Hesitation
- Avoidance

Instead of thinking freely, the child begins to think:

What if I get this wrong?

And that question limits everything.

When Fear Replaces Curiosity

Fear blocks learning.
When children fear mistakes:

- They stop trying new ideas
- They avoid difficult questions
- They stay within safe limits

Learning becomes mechanical.
Effort continues,
but connection is lost.

Bringing Meaning Back

Interest can return.
Not by forcing it—
but by restoring meaning.
Begin with small shifts:

- Connect learning to real life
- Encourage questions
- Allow time to think

When learning makes sense...
it becomes engaging again.

A Simple Shift

Instead of asking:
Did you complete your work?

Try asking:

- What did you understand best?
- What felt confusing?
- What would you like to explore?

These questions reconnect the child with learning.

Reflection

Pause and reflect:

- When was my child last excited to learn?
- What reduces their interest?
- Am I focusing on completion or understanding?

Try This (Simple Shift)

Over the next few days:

- Let your child explain concepts in their own words
- Reduce interruptions during thinking time
- Appreciate effort—even when incomplete

Observe what changes.

Key Takeaway

> Interest does not disappear by accident.
> It fades when meaning is lost—
> and returns when meaning is restored.

What This Shows

- Interest fades when learning loses meaning
- Pressure and fear quietly replace curiosity
- Compliance is not the same as learning
- Understanding grows when children feel safe to think
- Small shifts in questions can restore engagement

When meaning is lost, interest fades.
When meaning returns, learning begins again.

4 — From Reminders to Relationships

The more you remind,
the less they respond.

Why Reminders Stop Working

"Did you finish your homework?"
"Have you revised?"
"Why are you taking so long?"
These are familiar questions in most homes.
They come from care.
They come from responsibility.
But over time, something unexpected happens.
The more we remind,
the less children respond.

The Cycle of Reminders

At first, reminders feel helpful.
They keep children on track.
They ensure work gets done.

But gradually, a pattern forms:

- The parent reminds
- The child delays
- The parent reminds again
- The child responds only when pushed

Over time, this builds dependence.
Reminders create dependence.
Relationships build responsibility.

What Children Learn

When reminders become constant, children begin to believe:

- "I will act when I am told"
- "Someone else will keep me on track"

They stop initiating.
They start waiting.

Responsibility slowly shifts away from them.

A child who depends on reminders
is not learning responsibility.

Building Responsibility

If reminders don't work long-term, what does?
Connection.
A relationship built on:

- Trust
- Conversation
- Understanding

One of the simplest ways to build this connection
is through everyday family time.

A few minutes together—
during dinner or a short story before bedtime—
creates space for conversation.

When children talk about their day,
or what they are grateful for,
they begin to feel heard and valued.

These small moments build trust—
and that trust supports responsibility and learning.

Instead of managing tasks,
we begin to understand the learner.

Changing the Conversation

Instead of asking:
Did you finish your work?
Try asking:

- What did you learn today?
- What part did you enjoy?
- What felt challenging?

This focus then moves:

- from completion → to understanding
- from pressure → to engagement

When children feel heard,
they begin to take ownership.

Why Relationships Matter

A strong relationship creates:

- Emotional safety
- Openness
- Willingness to try

When children feel supported—not judged—they:

- Ask more questions
- Take initiative
- Build confidence

They begin to guide themselves.

Connection builds confidence.
Confidence builds independence.

A Practical Shift

Provide space, time and independence:

"Make your bed before breakfast."
"Tidy your room before going to bed."
These are not repeated reminders.
They are clear expectations with time and structure.

When Reminders Are Helpful

Not all reminders create dependence.
Clear, well-timed expectations can build responsibility.
They give children:

- Time to act
- Clarity of expectation
- Freedom to take responsibility

The difference is simple:
Repeated reminders create dependence.
Clear expectations build independence.

Key Takeaway

> Reminders may complete tasks.
> Relationships build responsibility.

The Shift

- Frequent reminders create dependence
- Children begin to wait instead of initiating
- Responsibility grows through trust, not control
- Conversations are more powerful than instructions
- Connection leads to ownership and independence

The more we connect, the less we need to remind.

5 — Empowerment vs Enforcement

Discipline is not built through control.
It is built by ownership.

What Truly Builds Discipline?

One of the most common questions parents ask is:

How do I make my child more disciplined?

The instinctive response is often:

- Set stricter rules
- Monitor more closely
- Enforce consequences

At first, this approach may seem effective—but only temporarily. But something important is missed.

What Enforcement Really Does

Enforcement focuses on control.

It sounds like:

- You must finish this now
- No excuses
- Do it because I said so

And yes, it produces results.

But those results are often short-lived.

Enforcement creates compliance.
Empowerment builds commitment.

The Limits of Control

When children act only because they are told:

- They depend on supervision
- They hesitate to act independently
- They struggle to self-direct

When supervision is removed, the behavior disappears.

What is controlled externally rarely lasts internally.

What Empowerment Looks Like

Empowerment shifts the message.
From:

- You have to do this

To:

- You are capable of doing this

It gives children:

- Ownership
- Responsibility
- Belief in their ability

The Power of Ownership

When children feel ownership:

- They plan their work
- They take initiative
- They follow through

Not because they are forced,
but because they choose to.

Ownership is the foundation of discipline.

A Practical Example

Instead of:

- "Study at 6 PM every day."
- "Finish your homework now."

Try:

- "Plan your study time for the week."
- "What does your timetable look like?"

The structure remains.
But now it is shared.
The child decides:

- When to study
- How to organize the week

Instead of:
"I was told to study..."
It becomes:
"This is my plan."

Why This Works

When children help create their routine:

- They feel responsible for it
- They think ahead
- They manage time better

Freedom in planning.
Responsibility in execution.

Balancing Freedom and Structure

Empowerment does not mean:

- No rules
- No expectations

It means:

- Clear expectations
- Shared decisions
- Gradual independence

Reflection

- Do I instruct or involve?
- Does my child act independently or only when told?
- Am I building compliance or commitment?

Try This

- Offer one choice instead of a command
- Ask your child to plan part of their study
- Trust them with small responsibilities

Observe what changes.

Key Takeaway

> Control may create short-term results.
> Empowerment builds long-term discipline.

What This Means in Practice

- Discipline grows from ownership, not control
- Enforcement creates compliance, not commitment
- Children need opportunities to decide and act
- Trust builds responsibility over time
- Small choices lead to strong independence

Ownership builds discipline.
Control only manages behavior.

6 — Creating a Learning Environment (Without Pressure)

Children don't just learn from books,
they learn from the environment.

Where Learning Really Happens

When we think about learning, we often focus on:

- Books
- Homework
- Study time

But learning is shaped by something deeper:
The environment in which it happens.

Beyond the Study Table

A learning environment is not just a desk or a quiet room.

It includes:

- The tone of conversations
- The expectations at home
- How mistakes are handled
- The emotional climate around learning

Even the best study setup cannot support learning if the environment feels stressful.

A calm environment supports focus.
A pressured environment blocks it.

When the Environment Creates Pressure

Without realizing it, pressure is created through:

- Constant reminders
- High expectations without support
- Comparisons with others
- Focus only on results

What follows is:

- Anxiety
- Hesitation
- Reduced confidence

The child may sit to study...
but not truly engage.

Present physically, but absent mentally.

What a Healthy Environment Looks Like

A positive learning environment is:

- Calm, not tense
- Supportive, not critical
- Encouraging, not demanding

It allows children to:

- Think freely
- Make mistakes
- Explore ideas

The Role of Emotional Safety

Emotional safety is essential.
When children feel safe:

- They ask questions
- They try new approaches
- They take learning risks

Learning grows where children feel safe to think.

Simple Ways to Improve the Environment

Small changes make a big difference.

1. Create a Calm Physical Space

- Keep the study area clean and organized
- Ensure proper lighting
- Reduce distractions

2. Set a Predictable Rhythm

- Maintain consistent study times
- Include breaks
- Avoid last-minute pressure

3. Change the Tone of Conversations

Instead of:
Why didn't you finish
Try:

- What was challenging today

4. Allow Time to Think

Give your child time to:

- Give space to process, reflect, and try independently

5. Balance Work and Rest

- Encourage breaks
- Ensure proper sleep
- Avoid overload

Rest is not separate from learning.
It supports learning.

Making Learning Visible

Bring learning into everyday life:

- Discuss ideas during daily routines
- Connect concepts to real situations
- Share what you are learning

This shows that learning is not limited to books.

Reflection

Pause and reflect:

- Does my child feel relaxed while learning
- Is the environment supportive or stressful
- What small change can I make today

Try This (Simple Shift)

Over the next few days:

- Reduce one source of pressure
- Introduce one calm routine
- Encourage one open conversation

Observe what changes.

Key Takeaway

> Pressure blocks learning.
> A calm environment builds it.

What This Looks Like

- Learning is shaped by the environment, not just content
- Emotional safety is essential for thinking and growth
- Pressure reduces engagement and confidence
- Small changes in space and tone create big impact
- Calm, consistent routines support deeper learning

A calm environment builds a focused mind.

7 — The 7 Building Blocks to A+

Big results are not built in a day.
They are built through small daily actions.

Where Change Begins

Learning is not just about effort—it is about direction.
Many students work hard but do not see results.
Because effort without structure does not lead to growth.
Instead of asking:
How much did you study?
Ask:
How are you learning?
Real progress comes from:

- Consistent habits
- Clear strategies
- Meaningful engagement

This is where the **7 Building Blocks** come in.

What Are the 7 Building Blocks?

Each one is small on its own.
Together, they create powerful change.
They help students:

- Understand better
- Remember longer
- Think independently
- Build confidence

The 7 Building Blocks

1. **Micro Reviews** — Recall to strengthen memory
2. **Teach-Back Technique** — Explain to deepen understanding
3. **Challenge Folder** — Learn from difficult problems
4. **Weekly Deep Dives** — Explore beyond routine learning
5. **Learning Journal** — Reflect and track progress
6. **Rest and Balance** — Recharge to improve focus
7. **Two Book Rule** — See concepts from multiple perspectives

Why These Work

These habits are effective because they:

- Focus on understanding, not memorization
- Encourage active learning
- Build consistency
- Develop independent thinking

Instead of depending on reminders, students begin to guide themselves.

From Effort to System

Motivation changes.
Habits stay.

When learning becomes a system:

- Stress reduces

- Clarity improves
- Results follow

Small actions, repeated daily, create lasting success.

The Role of Parents

Parents do not need to manage everything.
They need to:

- Introduce structure
- Encourage consistency
- Support reflection

The goal is not control—it is independence.

A Simple Start

You do not need to apply all seven at once.
Start small:

- Choose one habit
- Practice it daily
- Build consistency

Progress grows step by step.

A Walk, A Question... A Spark of Learning

One evening, on a simple walk home, I asked:
"What did you learn today?"

There was a pause.
Then the answer:
"Solutions... and mixtures."

I asked:
"How is a solution formed?"

Another pause.
Longer this time.
No clear answer.
And that was perfectly fine.
Because something important had just begun.

From One Question to Deep Learning

A Journey Through the 7 Building Blocks
A simple question can lead to deep learning—
when the right habits are applied.

1. Recall (Micro Review)
He tried to remember.
Learning returned to his thinking.

2. Understanding (Connection)
He came back with an example:
"It's like lemonade... sugar dissolving in water."
Now he was not just recalling—he was understanding.

3. Exploration (Two Book Rule)
He looked it up again, compared examples,
and thought more deeply.

4. Explanation (Teach-Back)
He explained it again—more clearly.
Understanding deepened.

5. Challenge
He asked:
"Are all solutions similar?"
Confusion led to deeper thinking.

6. Reflection (Learning Journal)
We wrote:
- What is a solution?
- One example
- One question

7. Deeper Learning (Weekly Deep Dive)
Over the weekend:
- Solute
- Solvent
- What does not dissolve?

8. Rest and Balance
We paused.
Learning needs space to grow.

The journey you explored can also be seen visually.
One simple question can activate all 7 Building Blocks.
The diagram below shows this complete learning cycle.

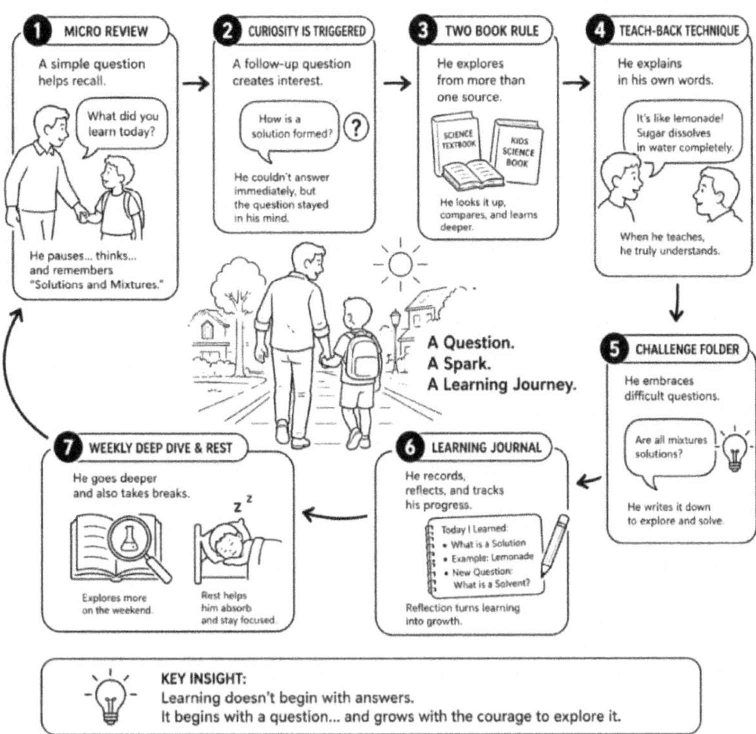

What This Shows

Learning happens:

- Without pressure
- Without constant instruction
- Through one simple question

One simple question activated:

- Recall
- Curiosity

- Exploration
- Explanation
- Reflection

*All **7 Building Blocks** were activated—naturally.*
A simple question can activate a complete learning system.

For Parents — Try This

You don't need to teach like a teacher — guide like a parent.

Ask simple questions:

- What did you learn today?
- Can you explain it in your own words?
- Where do we see this in real life?
- What part was confusing?
- What would you try differently next time?
- Can you think of another example?

Encourage:

- Thinking
- Recalling
- Explaining
- Exploring

Avoid:

- Giving immediate answers
- Turning it into a test
- Expecting perfection

Reflection for Parents

Pause and think:

- Did my child *recall* or just *repeat*?
- Did I ask questions or gave answers?
- Did learning continue beyond homework?

Key Insight

A single question can do what hours of study cannot.
It can:

- Ignite curiosity
- Build confidence
- Create independent learners

Small questions create big thinkers.

Closing Thought

Learning does not begin with answers.
It begins with a question...
and grows with the courage to explore it.
Try this: Ask one question today—and observe how your child thinks.

Key Takeaway

> Success is not created by intensity.
> It is created by consistency.

The Framework

- Strong learning comes from habits, not just effort
- Small daily actions create long-term results
- Structure brings clarity and reduces stress
- Consistency is more powerful than motivation
- Independence grows through guided habits

Small habits, practiced daily, create powerful results.

8 — How to Help Your Child Study Without Sitting Next to Them

True learning begins
when guidance turns into self-direction.

Why Independence Matters

The goal of learning is not just completion—
it is independence.
A child should be able to think, plan, and act without constant support.
Real success comes when:

- No one is reminding
- No one is supervising
- No one is pushing

And yet... learning continues.

The Common Challenge

Many children:

- Study only when told
- Stop when guidance is removed
- Wait for instructions

Over time, dependence begins to form.
Work may get done—
but the child is not leading their learning.

What Independent Learning Looks Like

An independent learner:

- Starts work without being told
- Plans how to approach tasks
- Tries before asking for help
- Reflects on what they understand

Not perfect—but responsible and engaged.

Why It Doesn't Happen Automatically

Independence is not built by leaving children alone.
It is built gradually through:

- Guidance
- Structure
- Trust

Too little support leads to confusion.
Too much control creates dependence.
Balance is key.

The Shift: From Support to Self-Direction

Move from:

- Doing things *for* the child

To:

- Thinking *with* the child

Instead of saying:

- Solve this question

Try asking:

- How would you start?
- What is your plan?

This shift builds ownership.

A Real-Life Moment

A parent sat beside their child every day during homework. Every step needed help.

One day, they stepped back.

"Start your work. I'll check in soon."

There was hesitation—but the child began.

Later, instead of correcting, the parent asked:
"What did you try?"

It wasn't perfect.
But it was independent.

Over time:

- Less waiting
- More trying
- More thinking

The child was still supported—
but no longer dependent.

Building Independence

Start small.

1. Ownership of Time

Let the child decide when to begin.
Encourage consistency.

2. Planning

Ask: "What is your plan?"

3. Productive Struggle

Pause before helping.
Let them attempt first.

4. Reflection
What worked? What can improve?
Small steps. Daily practice.

The Role of Mistakes

Mistakes are part of learning.
They help children:

- Think deeper
- Adjust strategies
- Build confidence

Without mistakes, there is no real growth.

When Independence Grows

- You will notice:
- They start on their own
- Stay focused longer
- Solve more independently

They begin to trust themselves.

Try This (Independence Through Small Projects)

Over the next few days, begin with simple shifts:

- Let your child plan their study
- Pause before helping
- Ask them to explain their thinking

Then, extend this into a small weekend project.

Weekend Project Ideas

- Complete a large puzzle together (1000+ pieces or more)
  Encourages planning, patience, and persistence

- Plan a one-week family vacation
  Destination, budget, and schedule
  Builds decision-making and ownership

- Organize a personal space or study area
  Teaches structure and responsibility

- Screen-Time Research Project: Animal Adaptations
  Choose one animal and explore:
  How it survives, where it lives, and key adaptations
  Present findings in your own words
  Turns screen time into active learning

STEM Exploration Project: Dinosaurs in Canada

Explore and Create
Visit or research a Canadian dinosaur site such as Dinosaur Provincial Park or the Royal Tyrrell Museum.
Find out what dinosaurs were discovered, how fossils are formed, and what paleontologists do.

Build a 3D Model
Choose a dinosaur and create a simple model using clay, cardboard, recycled materials, or a basic digital tool.
Include its name, habitat, time period, and one unique feature.

Learning Outcome

- Connects research with hands-on creation
- Builds curiosity, creativity, and problem-solving
- Encourages independent exploration and presentation

What to Focus On

- Let them take the lead
- Avoid step-by-step instructions
- Allow mistakes and adjustments
- Encourage planning and reflection
- Build confidence through trust

Key Takeaway

> Independence is built step by step.

Support builds confidence.
Confidence builds independence.

9 — The Power of Micro Reviews and Teach-Back

What we revisit, we remember.
What we explain, we understand.

Why Learning Is Forgotten

Many children study regularly, but forget quickly.
Why?
Because learning is often:

- One-time
- Passive
- Focused on completion

Without reinforcement,
information fades.

What Are Micro Reviews?

Micro Reviews are short, frequent revisits of learning.
Not long study sessions.
Just a few minutes to recall.
They help children:

- Strengthen memory
- Retain concepts longer
- Build clarity over time

Learning improves when it is revisited.

How Micro Reviews Work

Instead of rereading notes, encourage recall.
Ask:

- What do you remember from today
- Can you explain this without looking

This activates the brain.
And what is recalled...
is remembered.

The Power of Teach-Back

Teach-Back means explaining what you learned in your own words—to anyone.
When children explain:

- Gaps become visible
- Understanding deepens
- Confidence grows

Why This Method Works

Micro Reviews and Teach-Back:

- Turn passive learning into active learning
- Strengthen memory through recall
- Build deeper understanding
- Encourage independent thinking

This is not more study.
It is better study.

A Simple Daily Practice

No extra time needed.

- 5 minutes of recall after study
- Explain one concept daily
- Review key ideas before sleep

Consistency matters more than duration.

A Simple Example

A child is asked:
How many different 4-digit numbers can be formed from 1, 2, 3, and 4?

Instead of listing randomly, think step by step:

- 4 choices for the first place
- 3 for the next
- Then 2, then 1

Total:
$4 \times 3 \times 2 \times 1 = 24$

This is not just an answer—
it is a method.

Where Micro Review Begins

Later, ask:

"Do you remember how we solved it?"

The child pauses... recalls:
"4 choices... then 3, then 2, then 1..."

That short recall is a **Micro Review.**
The idea strengthens.

Now Comes Teach-Back

Ask:

"Can you explain it?"

The child says:
"We are arranging digits. Each place has fewer choices, so we multiply."

That is **Teach-Back**.

Understanding becomes clearer.
Confidence begins to grow.

A Small Change

Now ask:

"What if the digits are 3, 2, 1, and 0?"

The child thinks.

A number cannot begin with 0.
So:

- First place: 3 choices only not 4
- Remaining: 3 × 2 × 1 = 6

Total: 18 valid numbers.

Now the child sees:
The method is the same—
but thinking must adjust.

What This Shows

Learning grows when children:

- Recall an idea
- Explain it
- Apply it to a new situation

This is the combined power of
Micro Review and Teach-Back.

Thinking Clues for Curious Conversations

You do not need to give every answer.
A thoughtful question can begin real learning.

Mystery of Light, Colour, and Heat
Q1. Why does the sky look red or blue?
Q2. Why is red used for the stop lights?
Q3. Why does a glass house stay warm longer?
Q4. Why do dark clothes feel hotter in sunlight?

Ask:

- What do you notice?
- What do you already know?
- Can you explain it another way?
- Does your answer fit what we observe?

A Deeper Connection — Magnets and Migration

Q5. How birds use Earth's magnetic field to find their way?

Many birds travel long distances
and still return to the same place.

Ask:

- What do you know about magnets and magnetic fields?
- Does Earth behave like a magnet?
- How might a bird sense direction during its journey?

These are not test questions.
They are thinking prompts.
They help children:

- Recall
- Explain
- Reflect
- Connect learning to real life

That is how understanding grows.

What Parents Can Do

You do not need to solve the problem. Just guide. Ask:

- How did you get that?
- Can you explain it another way?
- What changed in this example?
- Does your answer make sense?

These questions help children
recall, explain and think deeply.

The Real Learning

This is not just about mathematics.
It is about learning how to learn.
When children:

- Revisit ideas
- Explain their thinking
- Reflect on understanding

Learning becomes lasting.

The Role of Parents

Support by:

- Listening without interrupting
- Asking simple questions
- Encouraging explanation, not perfection

You don't need to teach. Just listen.

Common Mistake to Avoid

Do not:

- Turn this into a test
- Correct every mistake immediately
- Focus only on accuracy

Allow time for thinking, pause, and refinement.

When This Becomes a Habit

Children begin to:

- Recall naturally
- Explain clearly
- Reflect independently

Learning becomes stronger—and their own.

Reflection

Pause and reflect:

- Does my child review what they learn, or move on quickly?
- Do they explain ideas—or only read?

Try This

- Ask your child to explain one concept daily
- Encourage recall without looking
- Listen without correcting immediately

Observe what changes.

Key Takeaway

> Learning improves when we revisit and explain.
> Understanding grows when we actively engage.

Key Insight

- Memory strengthens through repeated recall
- Explaining builds deeper understanding
- Active learning is more effective than passive reading
- Small daily reviews create lasting retention
- Listening supports confidence and clarity

Do not just study more. Study smarter.

10 — Mistakes Are Not Failures — They Are Feedback

Every mistake carries a message—
if we are willing to listen.

The Fear of Mistakes

Many children believe:

- Getting it wrong means failure
- Mistakes reduce their ability
- Errors should be avoided

So, they stop trying.
And when they avoid mistakes...
they avoid growth.

What Mistakes Really Mean

A mistake is not failure.
It is information.
It shows:

- What is not yet understood?
- Where thinking needs adjustment?
- What to improve next?

Mistakes are not the end—they are part of learning.

When Perfection Becomes a Problem

If only correct answers matter:

- Children hesitate
- They avoid challenges
- They play safe

Learning looks perfect,
but understanding remains shallow.

A Better Question

Instead of:
Why did you get this wrong?
Try:

- What did you learn here?
- Where did the thinking change?
- What will you try next?

As a result, the focus moves from judgment → to learning.

A Simple Home Moment

A child gets a math problem wrong.
Instead of correcting it immediately,
the parent asks,
"Can you walk me through your steps?"

The child finds the error, fixes it,
and solves the next one correctly.
The mistake didn't stop learning—
it guided it.

A Simple Example

A child writes in a test:
$2^0 = 0$
At first glance, it looks like a mistake.
But it is also an opportunity to understand.

Consider:

- $2^3 = 2 \times 2 \times 2 = 8$
- $2^2 = 2 \times 2 = 4$
- $2^1 = 2$

Ask:
What do you notice?
As the exponent decreases by 1,
the value is divided by 2.
So:
$2^1 = 2$
$2^0 = 2 \div 2 = 1$

Now ask:
What might 2^{-1} be?
Pause.
Let the child think.

What This Shows
The mistake was not a failure.
It was a starting point.

With the right question,
a wrong answer becomes understanding.

Learning from Others

It is important to learn from your own mistakes—
but also from the mistakes of others.

Simple conversations at the dinner table
can become powerful learning moments.

Share situations like:

- Getting on the wrong bus
- Preparing for the wrong test
- Picking up the wrong bag

Ask:

- What went wrong?
- What could be done differently?

These small discussions build awareness and better decisions.

Turning Mistakes into Growth

1. Identify the mistake
2. Understand why it happened
3. Correct it independently
4. Try a similar question

This builds clarity, confidence, and independence.

The Role of Parents

Children learn how to view mistakes
by watching us.

- Stay calm
- Ask, don't react
- Encourage retry

Focus on effort, not just results.
The goal is not to avoid mistakes—
but to learn from them.

When Fear Disappears

When mistakes feel safe:

- Children try more
- Think deeper
- Take learning risks

And that is where real growth begins.

Reflection

- How does my child react to mistakes?
- How do I respond when they get it wrong?
- Do we treat mistakes as failure or feedback?

Try This (Simple Shift)

Over the next few days:

- Ask your child what they learned from a mistake
- Encourage retry instead of correction
- Appreciate effort, even when incorrect

Notice the shift.

Key Takeaway

> Mistakes are not failures.
> They are feedback for growth.

The Real Impact

- Mistakes reveal gaps in understanding
- Fear of mistakes limits learning
- Reflection turns errors into improvement
- Growth comes from trying, not avoiding
- Confidence builds when mistakes are accepted

Every mistake is a step forward—if we learn from it.

11 — From Average to A+ — What Actually Changes

Improvement is not a sudden leap.
It is a series of small, consistent shifts.

The Common Belief

Many students believe:

- Some are naturally good at studies
- Others are not

So average results feel permanent.
But they are not.

What Really Changes

Moving from average to A+ is not about more hours.
It is about better habits.
A shift in:
• How you learn

- How you think
- How you approach challenges

The Real Difference

High-performing students are not always more talented.
They are more:

- Consistent
- Reflective
- Structured

They follow systems—not just effort.
One such system is a simple **Learning Ledger**— a record of what is learned, reviewed, and improved over time.
What gets recorded gets improved.

From Doing More to Doing Better

Average learning:

- Rereading
- Finishing tasks
- Last-minute study

Effective learning looks like:

- Regular review
- Explaining ideas
- Learning from feedback

What follows is a subtle but powerful shift:

From doing more → to doing better.

Think Beyond — What Actually Changes in Practice

Understanding the shift is important.
Seeing it in action makes it real.

As a teacher, I often notice this:

Some questions are not difficult...
they are simply unfamiliar.

This is where A+ students stand out.

Example 1 — Equation of a Line
Most students can:

- Find the equation using slope and a point
- Use two points
- Read from a graph

But very few answer:
What is the equation of the y-axis?

$$x = 0$$

The challenge is not the concept—
it is seeing beyond standard forms.

Example 2 — Extending Understanding
Can the square of a number be smaller than the number itself?
Many say "No," thinking only of whole numbers.
But:

$$\left(\frac{1}{2}\right)^2 = \frac{1}{4}$$

The limitation is not ability—
it is restricted thinking.

Example 3 — Real-Life Connection
Two students learn about **heat and temperature**.

One student memorizes:
"Heat flows from a hot object to a cold object."

In a test, they write the definition correctly.

Another student says:
"When I hold an ice cube, my hand feels cold
because heat is leaving my hand and going into the ice."

The difference is clear:
One **recites the idea**.
The other **experiences and explains it**.

What Actually Changes?

Average approach:

- Stays within practiced examples
- Focuses on completing work

A+ approach:

- Explores beyond the question
- Applies ideas in new situations
- Connects learning across topics

The Real Shift

From:

- Following methods

To:

- Understanding concepts

From:

- What was taught

To:

- What is possible

Simple Insight
A+ students are not just solving problems.
They are **exploring ideas**.

Try This

Ask one question daily:

- “Can this work in another way?”
- “Where do we see this in real life?”
- “What happens if we change the condition?”

Key Takeaway

The move from average to A+
is not about doing more.

It is about **seeing more**
in the same problem.

Small Habits, Big Results

Progress comes from small habits:

- Daily review
- Clear understanding
- Consistent practice

Tracking these in a Learning Ledger makes progress visible.

Confidence Follows Progress

As understanding improves:

- Confidence increases
- Fear reduces
- Effort becomes focused

Confidence is built through progress—not before it.

Consistency Over Intensity

Motivation changes.
Consistency stays.
Small daily effort
beats irregular bursts.

The Role of Parents

Support this shift by:

- Encouraging habits
- Reducing pressure
- Asking reflective questions
- Reviewing progress together

Focus on progress—not perfection.

Reflection

Pause and reflect:

- Does my child focus on effort or strategy
- Are habits consistent or irregular
- Do we track progress or only results

Try This (Structured Approach)

- Focus on one concept deeply
- Review one topic daily
- Reflect on one mistake
- Record learning in a **Learning Ledger**

Encourage variety:

- Choose concepts from different subjects
- Go deeper in at least one area
- Occasionally discuss current events or global ideas

Watch the change.

Key Takeaway

> Success is not a result of ability alone.
> It is built through habits, strategy, and consistency.

What This Leads To

- Small changes create big results
- Strategy matters more than effort alone
- Habits create long-term success
- Confidence grows through understanding
- Consistency is stronger than motivation

Do not aim to do more.
Aim to do better—consistently.

12 — From Success to Leadership — Raising Thinkers

Success shows what a child can achieve.
Leadership shows who they become.

Beyond Marks and Achievement

Academic success builds:

- Confidence
- Opportunities
- Direction

But the deeper question is:
What kind of learner is your child becoming?

Success vs Leadership

Success is about:

- Scores

- Performance
- Personal results

Leadership is about:

- Independent thinking
- Responsibility
- Impact

Success measures results.
Leadership shapes identity.

What Leaders Do Differently

Children who grow into leaders:

- Ask deeper questions
- Think beyond instructions
- Explain to others
- Take initiative

They are not just learners.
They become contributors.

How Leadership Begins

Leadership starts early:

- Explaining a concept
- Asking "why"
- Taking ownership

Small actions build identity.

Example — From Learning to Leading (At Home)
A child learns about the **water cycle** in school.
They remember the steps—
evaporation, condensation, precipitation—
and do well on the test.
At home, while cooking, they notice steam rising.
They say:
"This is like evaporation...
and when water forms on the lid, that's condensation."

Later, a sibling asks,
"What does this mean?"
The child explains it using the same example.

The shift is simple:
From **learning for oneself**
to **helping others learn**.

This is how leadership begins—
in small, everyday moments.

The Power of Thinking
Not just: *What is the answer?*
But:

- Why does it work?
- What can improve?
- What else is possible?

Thinking creates awareness.
Awareness creates leadership.

The Role of Parents

Encourage:

- Questions
- Ideas
- Reflection

Focus not only on performance—
but on perspective.

A Simple Shift

Instead of: Did you do well?
Ask:

- What did you learn?
- Can you explain it to someone?
- What new idea did you find?

This shift builds awareness and purpose.

When This Transformation Happens

When children:

- Think independently
- Learn consistently
- Reflect deeply

They no longer study just for marks.
They grow into thinkers.
And thinkers become leaders.

Reflection

- Is the focus only on results?
- Or also on thinking and understanding?
- Does my child help others learn?

Try This (Simple Shift)

- Ask your child to teach one idea?
- Encourage thoughtful questions
- Appreciate initiative—not just achievement

Notice the shift.

Key Takeaway

> Success is important.
> Leadership is transformational.

What This Means For Your Child

- Leadership grows from thinking, not just achievement
- Learning should lead to contribution
- Asking deeper questions builds awareness
- Confidence expands when children help others
- Education should shape thinkers—not just performers

Do not just prepare your child for exams.
Prepare them to think, lead, and grow.

From Curiosity to Leadership — The Journey So Far

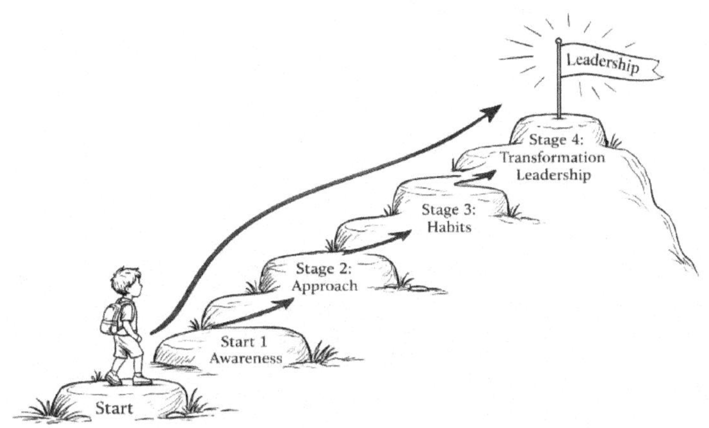

From Curiosity to Leadership — A Journey of Small, Meaningful Shifts

---

Curiosity begins the journey of learning.
Leadership is built when learning turns into *action.*

Every child starts curious—asking, exploring, trying to understand.
But without direction, curiosity fades.
With guidance, it grows into confidence, independence, and purpose.
These 12 chapters form one connected journey—
from dependence to independence...
from success to leadership.
This final chapter brings it all together—
so learning is not just achieved, but lived.

The 4-Stage Transformation Model

Stage 1 — Understanding the Problem *(Chapters 1–3)*
We begin by recognizing what is often unseen.

- Learning struggles are not about ability
- They are about **how learning is experienced**

Children lose confidence not because they cannot learn—but because curiosity is replaced by pressure.
The shift begins with awareness.

Stage 2 — Changing the Approach *(Chapters 4–6)*
Once we understand the problem, we change how we guide.

- From reminders → to relationships
- From control → to empowerment
- From pressure → to environment

Children do not grow through force.
They grow through connection, trust, and safety.
The shift moves from control to guidance.

Stage 3 — Building Effective Habits *(Chapters 7–9)*
With the right environment, we build the system.

- The 7 Building Blocks create structure
- Independence begins to develop
- Learning becomes active (recall, explain, reflect)

Children move from: Passive learning → to active thinking
The shift moves from effort to effective learning.

Stage 4 — Creating Transformation *(Chapters 10–12)*
That's where real growth happens.

- Mistakes become feedback
- Average becomes A+ through better methods
- Success evolves into leadership

Children begin to:

- Think independently
- Reflect deeply
- Contribute meaningfully

The shift moves from performance to purpose.

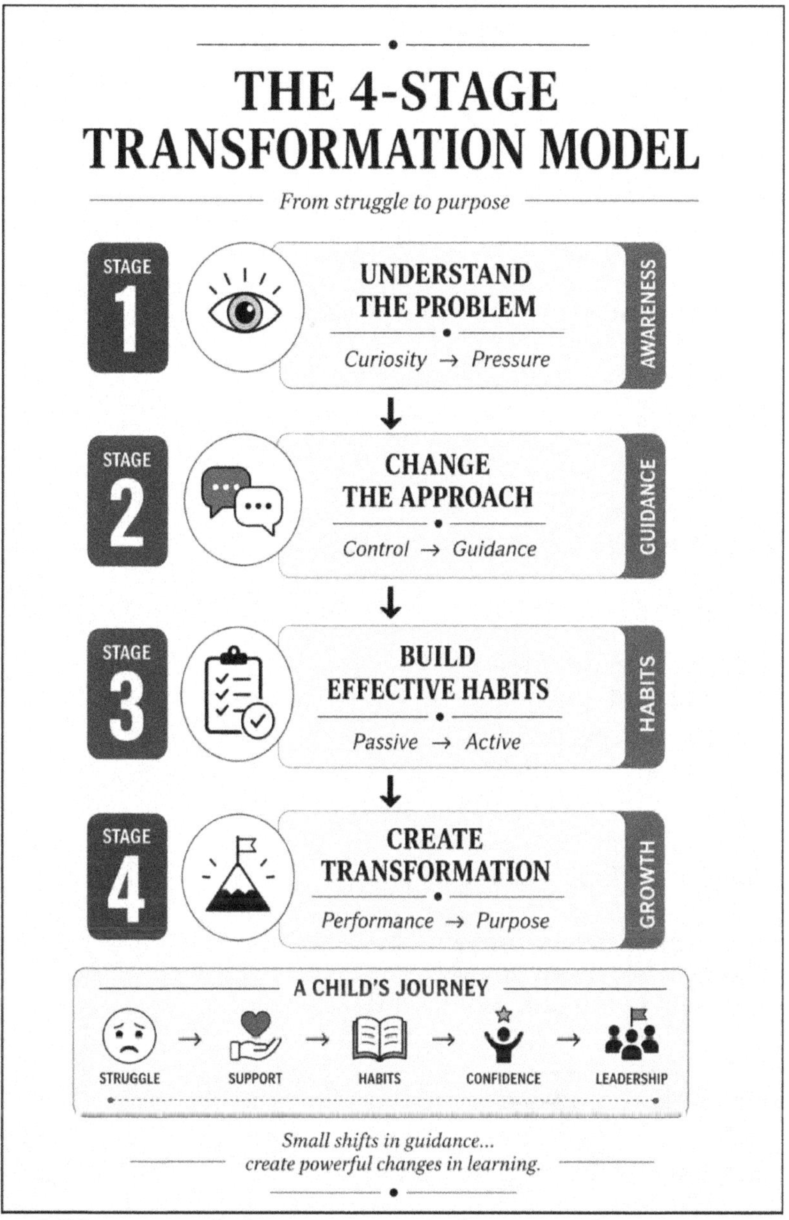

A child once needed constant reminders to study.
With better guidance and small habits,
they began to plan, explain, and think independently.
The real change was not in effort—
but in how they approached learning.

The Complete Transformation

From this journey, a clear progression emerges:

From	**To**
Pressure	Guidance
Marks/Grades	Curiosity
Dependence	Independence
Memorizing	Thinking
Performance	Leadership

Structured Progression

By applying these principles, your child will:

- Learn with confidence
- Think with clarity
- Study independently
- Approach challenges with resilience
- Grow into a thoughtful, capable individual

The Core Idea

As we saw in the examples,
success is not about doing more.
It is about doing things differently.

What Comes Next

Now it is time to move from understanding to action.
The following worksheets will help you:

- Apply these ideas in daily learning
- Build consistent habits
- Track progress over time

Your Learning Reflection Workbook

Learning begins with understanding…
transformation happens through action.

Turning Ideas into Action

- Reflect on your current approach
- Apply key ideas from each chapter
- Track your progress
- Build lasting habits

How to Use This Workbook

- Complete one section at a time
- Be honest in your responses
- Focus on progress—not perfection

Consistency matters more than intensity.

Section A: Core Reflection

- How does my child approach learning?
- When are they confident or hesitant?
- Am I focusing more on marks or understanding?
- Is the learning environment calm and supportive?

Action

- Ask one "why" question daily
- Improve one study habit
- Create a simple routine
- Step back gradually to build independence

Your Notes

Section B: Growth & Habits

Growth Focus

- Which habit is strong?
- Which habit needs improvement?
- How does my child respond to mistakes?
- How can I encourage independent thinking?

Action

- Focus on ONE habit this week — keep it simple
- Replace correction with guidance
- Encourage reattempt
- Ask one thinking-based question daily

Your Notes

Weekly Learning Tracker

Focus Area	What Worked	Improve

This Week's Focus

What I Will Do Daily

How I Will Measure Progress

Final Reflection

What is one change I made that created the biggest impact?

Download Your Learning Workbook

Scan the QR code to access the printable workbook:

One day, your child will not need your reminders... but they will carry your guidance for life.

www.ingramcontent.com/pod-product-compliance
Lightning Source LLC
LaVergne TN
LVHW011049110826
845149LV00015B/3425

* 9 7 8 1 0 6 9 3 8 6 2 5 0 *